Praise for Dan Fante

The Fantes, father and son, have been a major new discovery for me in these last few years.

—John Fowles

Dan Fante. Remember the name.

—Kevin Ring, *Beat Scene*

Fante offers moments which brush the genius of Bukowski and Hubert Selby, Jr.

—*Elle*

. . . in his eyes there's his obsession: words.

—*Backbeat*

Praise for *Chump Change*

Excruciatingly raw.

—*LA Weekly*

Chump Change is grotesquely readable, full of quiet horror and broad melancholy.

—*Beat Scene*

Bruised, corrosive and utterly compelling, *Chump Change* aches with Fante's sozzled wisdom, haggard philosophy and low-life compassion. It's a desperate yet desperately humane book.

—Kevin Sampson,
author of *Awayday and Powder*

On one level, with the air and vapors of Fitzgerald on every page, this book might appear to be merely another account of America hits the bottle. But *Chump Change* is better than that, and its nihilistic undertones are offset by a genuine filial affection at the heart, and a wit which does not disguise the deathly kismet that is the boozer's lot.

—*Literary Review*

In the end, you get an unforced and utter human story . . . read it.

—*MAXIMUMROCKNROLL*

Praise for *Mooch*

Dark and bleak, dirty and real . . . Dan Fante's style is raw, insightful and deftly realized.

—*Time Out*

Mooch transcends the genre's staple macho Bukowskian antics with brutal honesty and painful vulnerability.

—*LA Weekly*

Fante's soul-bearing battle with his demons, coupled with his bull-shit-free outlook make for compulsive, life-affirming reading.

—Ben Myers, *Kerrang*

A violent lyrical blizzard of alcoholic despair.

—*Uncut*

Praise for *Boiler Room*

Powerful . . . strong . . . sexy. A requiem for those who have made fatal choices and carried false values.

—*Los Angeles Tribune*

Fante's play about power and sex-driven telemarketers electrifies.

—*Los Angeles Times* Best Bet

A gin-pissing-raw-meat-dual-carburetor-V8-son-of-a-bitch from Los Angeles

collected poems
1983-2002

Dan Fante

original art by Michael Napper

Foreword by Joyce Fante

Introduction by Ben Pleasants

2002
Sun Dog Press
Northville, Michigan

Cover design by Grey Christian

Book design by Judy Berlinski

The publisher wishes to thank Judy Berlinski for her professional help in the preparation of this book.

Library of Congress Cataloging-in-Publication Data

Fante, Dan, 1944-

A gin-pissing-raw-meat-dual-carburetor-V8-son-of-a-bitch from Los Angeles : collected poems, 1983-2002 / Dan Fante ; original art by Michael Napper ; foreword by Joyce Fante ; introduction by Ben Pleasants.

p. cm.

ISBN 0-941543-31-5 (alk. paper) — ISBN 0-941543-32-3 (signed : alk. paper)

1. Los Angeles (Calif.)—Poetry. I Title.

PS3556.A545 G5 2002
811'.54—dc21

2002029209

Printed in the United States of America

This book is dedicated to the brilliant Jolene Adams of The Actors Art Theater in Los Angeles. My friend . . . and fearless coconspirator.

Foreword

Joyce Fante

In the not-so-gentle hands of Dan Fante, poetry is more akin to surgery or the body shop than to the techniques of music and painting. Fante excises whole slices of life and lays them bare for us to inspect. Pain and self-mocking humor are the writer's tools here. He pries open and exposes his heart with the kindness of a hammer or crowbar. Indeed, what could be more ego-sizing than to have all pretense flattened, laying bare the raw self underneath?

To quote:

"Until my brain was burning through my hair and eating me alive and until walking and talking and putting on my shoes and trying to write and breathing in and out—all of it was killing me and I hurt so bad I didn't want to spend another five minutes in my skin."

No other living poet I know writes like this. Fante's distinctive view and voice erupt off each page. Read other writers as you will, but know this: you will never feel the same after opening this book.

Introduction

Ben Pleasants

For the straight male writer, L.A. is an unforgiving kind of town.

On the one hand, there's Hollywood where fists full of cash are plunked down each day on silly sitcom and bad action flicks and the well-paid scribbler knuckles under, does what he's told, banks his cash and moves up into the hills hoping to become a producer; on the other hand, there's nothing. Forget Guggenheim fellowships and the patrons from Little Old Lady Land: what's out there is the hot sun, shit jobs at minimum wage, bad marriages and unemployment checks.

Only Los Angeles could have produced writer like Nat West, John Fante, Raymond Chandler and Charles Bukowski. Their hard prose has rewritten the American language, spilling over into the rebirth of real language poetry.

Dan Fante was born of them and moved among them, and only Los Angeles could have produced a Dan Fante.

His novels, his plays, and his poetry are all barbed wire bouquets of rage against the drabness of conformity. His life and his writings are like the square root of minus one: they challenge the imagination and like his father John Fante and the poet Charles Bukowski, he has been neglected in his own country.

Now Sun Dog Press, who first published his novel *Chump Change* in America, lays down twenty years of Dan Fante poetry, with the personal illustrated diaries and fascinating drawings by his friend Michael Napper.

A gin-pissing-raw-meat-dual-carburetor-V8-son-of-a-bitch from Los Angeles comes roaring at you like a river of fire straight from hell.

All the essence of his life and work he packed into these one hundred and twenty-eight pages: bad marriages, early love, the sadness of his father's house, diving down into the drunken depths of loneliness, abandoned cars, abandoned homes, abandoned lives as he sets out to make his way as a writer in Los Angeles.

"All I had to my name was my rage/and my father's temperamental Smith Corona," says Fante (p. 42). "Wives come and go/but a good used car/is a treasure" (p. 73).

Year by year we follow him down, down, down into the rat hole of loneliness and poverty that finally ends in attempted suicide and in the whittling down of self, the stripping away of ego and the final confrontation with his demons.

All the junk yard years are there in flaming day glow and they read more like Rimbaud than Bukowski. Dan Fante's *Drunken Boat*. Young readers may find themselves stuck where he was once, "We did hours in bed and I could never get enough (p. 79)." "About one day in ten/gun loaded—100 Secanol and a glass of water in front of me (p. 74); but it's the final poems, the ones that lead him back to the ghost of his famous father who he never stopped loving, but could never seem to please, or stumbling home to Malibu with "all that I own in a plastic bag," that reunites him with his family, takes him humbly to AA, and drives him back to the beginning of his being to find the solution to the problems of his life, the square root of minus one; these are the poems that moved me the most,

In his coda entitled "2000," Dan Fante say it best:

this voice that has survived shrinks and jails and 3 divorces and
suicide and bankruptcy and dozens of self-improvement week-
ends
this rage
still guides my vision
and demands that I go headfirst against my life
like a fool
in search of
a
pure
white
flame

I first met Dan Fante in his father' house in the late Seventies while doing a profile for the *Los Angeles Times Book Review.*

"He's trying to be a writer," John Fante said. I nodded, though he couldn't see me.

The last time I saw Dan Fante was at his father's funeral. I've seen him lately and I've read his books and I want to tell you, John, you don't have to worry. Your kid is one hell of a writer. You can be proud of him now. He has his own name.

SANTA MONICA

It looks like the same ocean
but this is Santa Monica—not nirvana
sitting
squinting out at sunrise in a forty-dollar-a-day motel
by the sea
all expenses paid by the snoring girl in bed behind me
who bought the drinks last night
after I read some of my ten-year-old stuff from a wine-stained notebook
and
one more time
made of fine success at impersonating a real writer

my shit—remarkably—even sounds like me
before I lost my muse
and became a hopeless moron-hasbeen-talentless-retard
fuck
with a freight train roaring through my mind
chasing a ridiculous lost idea of literary perfection

But I warn you
I'm like a dented 1985 Ford
with a busted radiator,
a cracked windshield,
and 3 bald tires
speeding down the 405

Don't try to diss me or pass me or call my bluff
'cause—see
when I'm cornered
I can write like a gin-pissing-raw-meat-dual-carburetor-V8-son-of-a-bitch

even in Los Angeles

KATIE

Half drunk
and a fool
at 1:00 a.m. in the Tattle-Tail Bar

somehow, sitting back down,
on my way from the jukebox
my face brushed your hair
and cuzzled your perfume

and I said hi—and you and your girlfriend Ginger
both
smiled back

and we talked

and then you were cold and so you put on your fake leopard coat
before you went to the ladies room
and—not knowing for sure why—
I stole your keys off the bar
and made a secret hidden game in my hand of trying to guess which one
went to what door

then tasted them, rubbing my tongue over each one

And you and Ginger sipping your marguerita
and talking about breast augmentation and upgrading your jobs and
moving to San Diego

And when the time was right I leaned over and whispered something like
"I like your tits" and went for the kiss
because—see—I knew if I didn't get one—I'd be ahead anyway
because
you'll be calling a locksmith in half an hour
and I
all the way home, will be humming a BB King love song to myself

BAD NIGHT

I met the meanest
bastard starving cat
while sitting with a book
on a bench
smoking half a pack of Luckies
at Venice beach

He saw me and came up
white
filthy
with one green eye
and one yellow eye
and a fresh slash on his scarred ear

Angry as a wounded wolf
he kept his distance
and his look said, feed me or fuck off
that bench you're on is my territory

What he didn't know is that I know desperate too
and crazy
and what emptiness and aloneness and rage can do to you when you've got nothing but your own pain in your pockets and your home is a busted-out 1978 Pontiac stalled in an alley in West L.A. and the voice in your mind is carving you up and killing more of you off each day and you wake up and drink more rat-piss wine to keep you from instant madness and god becomes a guy coming out of the 7-11 handing you chump change toward another fucking jug and fear is your finest feeling and love is dead and all time is dead and even your eyes stink and your gut is bloated with the screaming voices of those you hate and the only real sanity there is can be found in the small miracle of sucking back one more drink

That mean white cat didn't know that I've been cut too

from the same cloth

the only difference between us
is ten years and a typewriter

Stuck on my novel and wasting time
I drove up Beachwood Canyon in the hills
today
under the
H o l l y w o o d
sign
                                        and felt
again
how it must have been seventy years ago for my old man and Nat West
and Fenton and Bill Faulkner and that pack of over-paid, restless,
and
disenfranchised script doctor movie hacks

Looking down through the soot I said out loud,
"You   wanted this?"
A
Spanish mansion on this hill—and fame
and hearing people whisper your name when you entered Musso's bar
and
blowjobs from not-quite actresses after the card game and too many
drinks at the garden of Allah

Then
I reminded myself
that what you really left
behind
carelessly, unintentionally
in these greedy hills
could never have been bought or sold

John Fante's gift to me
was
his
pure writer's heart

I don't need . . .

a biblical bearded Jesus
with shaved arm pits
and trimmed Beverly Hills goatee
where the price tag for sanity
comes around
faithfully in a glittering collection plate

Salvation like that takes too long

The voices consuming my brain
or saving me from myself
are yelling
right now

here
now

The magic I need to quiet the slashing
and the screaming and the murderer
within
me
must
arrive on time
at the intersection of
right here—right now

Living
raw
exposed to the magnetism of death and life
each instant

used up or born again
now
I'll take that
or

the bone yard
for fatuous pussies

Okay, that's it!
I've spent too much time thinking over this shit
plotting
mocking up previews of conversation after conversation
designed to get my point across
—making sure that you absolutely consider MY side

while you stay barricaded in the bedroom talking to that false silicone
bitch you call every time we fight

this relationship has come to require my full-time concentration
worse even than TV

and I can't get anything done

I know,
why not just admit I'm right
and
let's move on

From the start I could tell she didn't love him
you know—100%

or give too much of a fuck about anything that wasn't her priority
her parking ticket, *her* electric bill—
because instinctively, I could see
she knew
how to use
him

she was perfect—a transcendent mooch master

And I told him: people do and say what we need
to say and do
to get what it is we think we need

lies are our way of staying alive

So one day last week she's gone and he's on the phone and drunk and
saying how perfect it all was and that he can't understand what happened
and me
listening and listening
and
and grunting uh-huh occasionally
and
finally running out of cigarettes
and saying
"Well—hey Mike, I gotta go now"
and
hanging up and realizing once again that conviction is still the essential
sales component in bullshit

and all the time the smell of her there next to me in the bed

When I think about my pop—now
now that he's really famous
and people are finally saying about him what he knew
and told everybody anyway thirty years ago

I realize that he never really doubted his genius
that his rages and bitterness were all wars against life

little unrecorded nuclear detonations—territorial marking

And it was all the same to Pop

Life was a bitch

PARROTS

Broke again
and
carless
and hoping to mooch a free month in Malibu
I discovered that now there are wild parrots breeding on Point Dume
In Malibu

Big
loud noisy green fuckers
laughing in the high trees—following me up the road in the afternoon
sun from the highway
chattering their non-sense like an orchestra in warm-up chaos

This time I'm coming home with all that I own in a plastic bag
along with my typewriter and my taste for gin

Mom opened the door
and smiled when she saw me
and
that night we laughed about the parrots and talked on endlessly
about
Dickens and Rupert Brooke and Millay
and that jerk T.S. Elliot

And I went off to the spare bedroom
drunk on free gin
sad for my old man's fading ghost
and thanking Jesus there was one person left alive
who'd still listen to my
bullshit

This isn't a poem...
just a list...

1994 A view of the Mountain top... MAY

Saturday 28

"I can't lead a normal life," he said. "I keep having to look at (my) nature."

How to Watch a Hummingbird

shaking
betraying
adhesion
unseen
until
we see something

NICHOLAS JOSEPH FANTE

You jerk
now it's three years
since you guzzled your last quart of supermarket bourbon
and paraded your guts and blood
on the your kitchen floor
and
denied and lied
and
died
completely insured—utterly alone

as white as your wife's faultless starched bed sheets

I still can't conclude a purpose
or a meaning
or a hint of wisdom
or recognize any spiritual symmetry
that could permit such pain
and loss

All I know is that you were a bad drunk and a genius—forlorn and sad and bad-tempered

I just keep wishing I'd had my chance to say good-bye

Hey Jimmi!
after
ten years (jesus, it is that long) and a million more gin n' tonics
it still stalks my brain
this stuff about
you

My mind just spit out a new toothless reanimation
like finding a cracked photograph in the back of a desk drawer
reminding me again
of how I was once impossibly hooked
—I guess impaled is the better word—by someone
as wilfully beautiful as you

Trust me—I know fortified thoughts are forgeries
but
just now—your ghost smiled over at me
sitting here on my stool at the Sunset Saloon
looking out at a Venice Beach winter night and the wind flinging shit
across the sand
at god
and a fat shopping cart lady diving in the garbage for half-eaten fast food
and aluminum cans
twenty feet away

making me understand—finally
what I've been left with
is only the falseness of a scent—and my trusty frosted glass

a forgery

nothing close to my heart's truest resonance
of the love and pain and bloodshed we caused other
or the real fragrance
of
you

CYNTHIA

He painted that painting
says eee—especially for *you*
no gallery will ever have it
and l o o k—eee says, see, I even signed it (in his stupid frilly flourish)
and
flashing fat teeth

Now eee tells U how nice your new blouse looks
and you leer back and I realize this whole deal—him being here in the
middle of the afternoon—iz filled with effusive
greasedpigshit
lies

And
the blue
eee says—with his best leer—
on that corner of the canvas represents his purest expression of intimacy
and is the same (fucking) blue as the peacock wallpaper in our bedroom
        where it should go
            and
                                you hold the thing
                    against the pillow on the couch and we all evaluate
and I watch this shit like a chimpanzee licking his cock because art for
art's sake is not what brought his ass here today
especially to bbbbbbb with u
and
before I can grab my keys
and go to the movies
or the bookstore or wherefuckinever it is I am escaping to go to
because now I don't drink no more or slam no dope
and
—in that instant—see for myself—
that being married to you one more goddamn day will cost me my sanity
say
"well, I'll see you later"
then kiss your perfect lips good-bye

1995 49th day — 316 days follow

Summer Weather

SATURDAY 18 FEBRUARY

Laundry
– Call Tabitha and Zobias re: Tax forms!
– Mail bills
– Ltr to Laurin … Brazil?
– 1000 C's

up @ 8:00 a.m.! down to Laundromat, call to Dipeatia, read in L.A. Times small unworthy obituary on Alberto Burri!! Bought N.Y. Times to see if there was anything on him, but it was probably in yesterday's edition. L.A. Times getting away real news late as usual.

Bad TV Drawing

Dipeatia over, I fixed us breakfast, lounged in the sun, then later lounged in the bedroom, no whoopee though, still recovering from H. effects. Tired, was it last night's Bordeaux, or rising early?

No work on book, no "good" receiving (meaning the Dream)… just lounging, semi-sloth until work @ 7:00 pm

[got out various travel bags for Shawna to borrow for her and Swan's cross-country drive]

– Millei on message machine

Phone message from Swan

Get together on the 26th (evening) and the 3rd (a.m.) for bon voyage… she is having friends each make a tape for her and Shawna to listen to on their trip.

Work

In the back room, never fully satisfying, as most people want to sit out front… Everyone stressed and frenzied at work tonight, Zach ready to punch a few of the more obnoxious waiters demanding their drinks immediately.

Stop on way home (made 70¢) for Sunday N.Y. Times, then to bed to read… Nothing on Burri's death.

SAFE … THIS P… AND P… PRODU… CAUSE… OR CO… FOLLO…

…STRUCTIONS
KEEP REFRIGERATED OR FROZEN. THAW IN REFRIGERATOR OR MICROWAVE.
KEEP RAW MEAT AND POULTRY SEPARATE FROM OTHER FOODS. WASH WORKING SURFACES (INCLUDING CUTTING BOARDS), UTENSILS, AND HANDS AFTER TOUCHING RAW MEAT OR POULTRY.
COOK THOROUGHLY.
KEEP HOT FOODS HOT. REFRIGERATE LEFTOVERS IMMEDIATELY OR DISCARD.
…D FROM INSPECTED …ULTRY. SOME FOOD …TERIA THAT COULD …CT IS MISHANDLED … YOUR PROTECTION, … INSTRUCTIONS.

BACON

DATE	$/LB	NET WT.
FEB. 18.95	3.49	0.53

TOTAL PRICE

1.85

10-11-83

Yesterday
suddenly newly fired
again
and optionless
I
dragged my
humbled ass
back to the back bedroom of my mother's old, cold house

Forty-one years old
checkbook balance in the high two digits
dozens of failed jobs
and a box filled with the photographs of kids and ex-wives
and
not a clue as to what to do

now

I unpacked
my newest unpublished novel
my
two—or is it three by now—unproduced plays
my
hundreds of poems and my Ray Carver short stories
and
my
dirty laundry

Passing Mom in the hall her eyes looked away
maybe ashamed—certainly annoyed
at
a washed-up son who once was regarded by some
as having
potential

Then, with nothin' to do
I made a mug of coffee, found my cigarettes,

and took the long walk to the cliff above the ocean
and

there
cold on a rock
connected to the moment
looked out
just in time
to witness the presence
of
another perfect Malibu sunset

When my shift is almost done at four-thirty a.m.
after 75 to 100 asses have pounded
the back seat of the cab
and 12 hours
behind the wheel's gone by—my sweating back glued to the summer
vinyl
and
me
not ever taking a break
and pissing in a cardboard milk carton under the front seat
smokin' sixty Luckie Filters one after the other
Jimmy Reed and Tom Waits and John Lee Hooker on the boom box
("all night long—oh baby—all night long")
I
glide into the Central Park Drive
and head
north—uptown
windows open
shirt pocket stuffed with the night's wadded profits

free
letting my mind go—now traveling to wherever fancy has found me

impersonating
real
peace

At night
when we hump
sometimes when I can't concentrate and start losing interest
I go back twenty-five summers
in my mind and think of
Stinky
who
was nineteen when we met at night school
and loved my ratty shoes and clumsy cab driver poetry
and had never been in the sack with a white boy
and had the most faultless and soft black skin and the smallest waist
and her pops owned a gas station upstate
and she'd come to me on the New York Central
and spend the weekends in my room on 51st Street
sippin' Mad Dog 20-20 all night
with the bathroom in the hall—and zombie junkies every-fuckin'-where
my radio whispering WABC love myths hour by hour
and the most divine unquenchable nonstop heat for each other

So
on these nights—when I begin to lose interest and the magic with you
feels gone
Stinky is my secret weapon
remembering her—the way she celebrated sucking my dick
deeply
that smile that always said fuck me more
I
think reopen that perfection
and quietly—as we do it—thank her
for helping me through this tired third marriage

Yvonne was gone—I was cleaned out
all our accumulated dual property shit—(bank account, stereo, electric typewriter, TV, microwave and vacuum cleaner) gone too—with her
And after a couple of days on pink rose from Gristede's Market and no food and half a carton of cigarettes
Old Harvey from the two-bedroom facing front downstairs knocks on my door, comes in, flops on my couch, pours a glass of my wine for himself, and begins talking
Not really a conversation because I wasn't saying much—just Harvey who had a need to drink free wine and tell me this story to cheer me up
So, he says: my friend Don once found a broken pigeon—it flopped on the kitchen window sill of his farm in South Jersey
the bird had a broken wing
so Don used an ice-cream stick and tape to splint the wing and nurse the bird back to health—
Then—one day—weeks later—the weather is hot and Don's kitchen window is open—he turns his back and the ungrateful pigeon flaps away into the blue backyard sky never to return
I'm making it short here but Harv took more time and several glasses of wine to describe to me fully Don's loss—and the ridiculous expectations we all get and the ebb and flow of things in life and unrequited love 'n shit—
It was a good story and well-told and I paid attention to everything Harvey said because I knew there was a hook in there for me
But when the bottle was gone he stopped
"So, Jesus Christ, what happened?" I said, "in the end? I mean, thaz a heartbreaker—Don musta felt like hell, right?"
"Nah," says Harvey, "Don had a ten-gauge in his porch closet—one day he sees the fucking pigeon perched on a fence near his chickens—and blasts its ungrateful ass alla way to Asbury Park—

Then Harv says, "hey," his eyes on the empty bottle, "I got money—let's buy some more wine"

So we did

Seeing you
for the first time
my head spun like a white plate
and
stopped

smashing up against your illegal beauty

You
twenty-two
auditioning
standing there reading pages of my new play
saying "okay," to the director, "I'll do it that way"
and me sitting—stumped—stupid as a pencil
knowing only that I had to chew your dress off with my teeth
and lick you everywhere
and close my checking account
and leave my girl friend
and loose ten pounds
and marry you on a weekend ride to Rose Rita Beach

dumbstruck and drooling
completely in love

way before you walked over and said "hi, my name's Anna"

7-8-84

Everybody on the inside—in the know—
was aware
of Prince Sihanouk's greed—his power lust
and my advice, I felt, once again, went unheeded
of course
after that
Cambodia
ultimately
was lost

I must say here that history had born me out time and again

And of course LBJ wouldn't listen
too dogmatic, inflexible
and McNamara?
hawkish . . . pigheaded . . . a psycho dressed in a bow tie

Then Nixon
his biggest problem was that nihilistic egomaniac Kissinger
grandiosity obsessed the man
clearly
power-corrupted

still the blood-letting in Asia kept on

Many of my own personal sessions lasted until 3 or 4 a.m.
but I did learned patience
and always attempted to manage an air of fairness and good humor
with my subordinates
yet
sadly
the delicate balance of power remained skewed
during my administration of the entire war
from
my bar stool at the Blarney Stone
on the corner of 56th Street and Eighth Avenue

After a while you just get tired
of explaining things

people see you for what you are or they don't

why try to describe the fog on Venice Beach
or having a passion for the perfection of the 1957 Chevy
—who gives a shit—
either you are into fog and Chevys or you are not

For me the magic comes from the privilege of living itself
the undeserved gift
and being present right now
going head-first against the bricks
or simply sitting in a chair and marveling at the cause of breathing in and
breathing out

It is all improvising—theater—a complimentary ticket—
unpredictable
horrible
ridiculous
senseless
brutal
precious
and
inspiring

an adventure

I know that I may not be much—but I am all that I think about

As a kid I wanted to care about something
other than The Dodgers
fall in love with a red-haired cheerleader
get taller
join the union
switch from carburetors to fuel injection
and spend my Julys in Hawaii on vacation

then I started reading books
and getting drunk and going to jail

and landed in New York City
broke
on a dare
and wound up driving a cab for seven years
watching the junkies in the doorways in East Harlem
and the blue-eyed butchers coming back from Nam
kids
like me
from Indiana and Montana
with the faces of the blown-apart and the gunned down
dismembered yearbook center folds
glowing from their pink Proctor & Gamble cheeks

and
eventually
I understood

trust nothing

all government sucks
all religion sucks

real heroes
sleep alone listening only to the beat of their own wild heart

What came between
me
and
complete madness—living death
was
a crazy old man—a bad-tempered ex-biker named Bob
forty years off booze

He used to laugh and tell stories about running guys off the freeway
pulling 'em out of their cars and punching 'em stupid

He'd see me around—look in my eyes—
and stick his fat finger in my face and breathe on me with his stinking breath
and tell me—
he'd say, "ain't you tired yet—sick 'n tired of the pain?"

Fuck him!
I ignored him
until my brain was burning through my hair and eating me alive
and until walking and talking and putting on my shoes and trying to write
and breathing in and out
all of it
was killing me
and I hurt so bad
I didn't want to spend another five minutes in my skin

I found the old bastard in a coffee shop talking trash with two other guys
and I sat down and said
Jesus, man, what the hell do I do now?

And old Bob saw me—observed that I was bleeding from the eyes
and he said
"I think you're ready"

And that's when it happened
I gave up and asked another man for help

All it did was save my ass

We're friends
we talk on the phone a couple of times a week
about women and his crack addict brother
I see him at AA meetings
and he comes around sometimes
and sits at my kitchen table and drinks my coffee
and regularly makes me aware of how bad me smoking cigars is for me
and gets up and opens my fucking windows without any—permission
whatever
and
one day starts asking about my writing
    about my novels and about
    this play or that play
and
    how many rewrites did it take to finish my first book
    and how many publishers did I send it to
    and how much do they pay
and
one
day
he hands me a story—it is fifty pages—single spaced
and he wants me to read it and tell him what I think
because he's always wanted to be a writer
so I read it and tell him—I say—Don, one-to-ten it's a six
but keep going—keep at it
Hustler Magazine wasn't built in a day
and
Don goes home and calls me an hour later
in this rage
to tell me what an unfeeling prick I am
and
after we hang up I look across the room at my fat tabby cat Daisy
who is one hundred percent devoted to me
as long as I pet her when she demands it and feed her
exactly on time

and
I thank Jesus Christ
that how I feel about myself comes from me—a clear center—
from a fire I've lit by myself—through my own pain

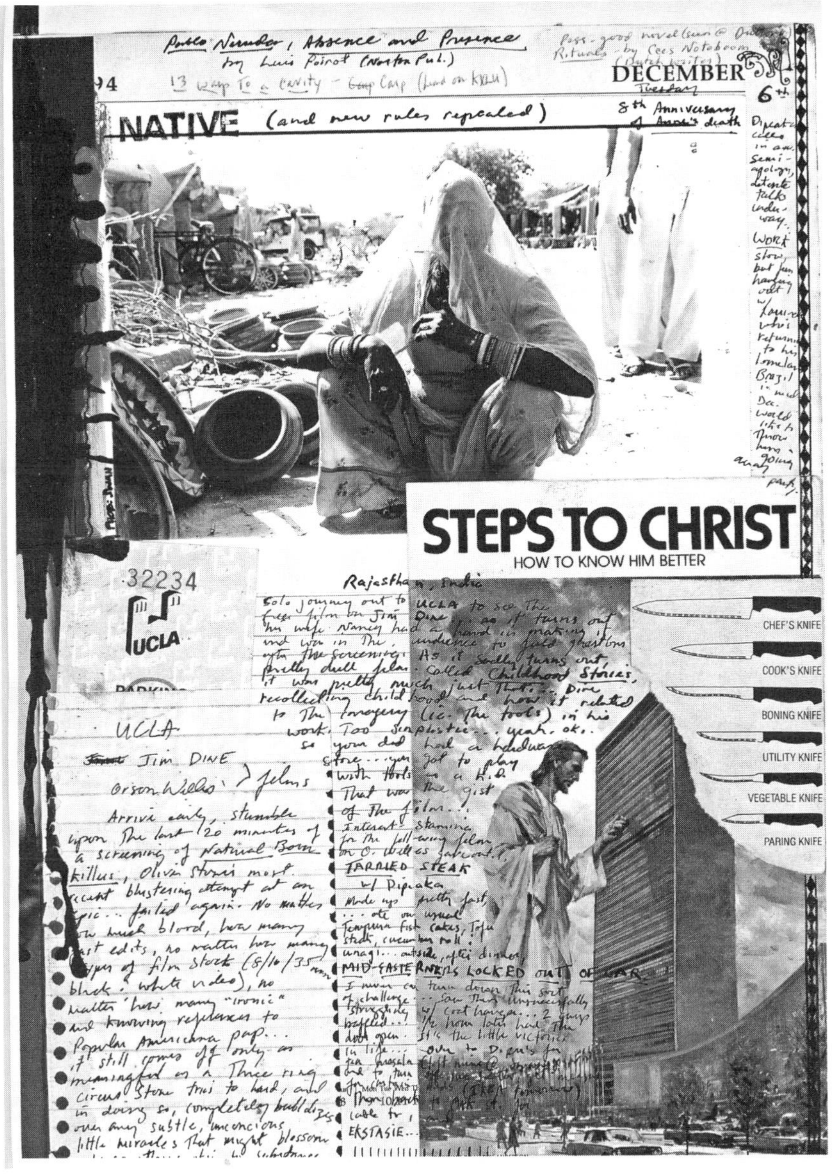

SONG

So drag your laundry down Rose Avenue
spend some time in your drugstore mind
it's not what you think, it's what you do
I've got a pair of socks I like better than you

I got me a clean shirt and my old pair of shoes
'n a '78 Chevy that'll get me from Venice Beach up to blue Santa Cruz
old Bob at the Alibi Room says a man's a fool makes the same mistake more'n twice
But Bob sits on that bar stool sippin' bourbon, eatin' peanuts, and callin' a TV fortuneteller to get advice

So drag your laundry down Rose Avenue
spend some time in your drugstore mind
it's not what you think it's what you do
I've got a pair of socks I like better than you

I'm packin' up my gear—my rusty typewriter and all I own
and I'm leavin' after midnight and not tellin' no one where I'm going
when you wake up I might be in Stockton or even lonesome San Rafael
gonna meet me a fat waitress, buy a bottle, forget about your face at the No-Smell-Motel

I said drag your laundry down Rose Avenue
then spend some time in your drugstore mind
it ain't what you think it's what you do
I had me a parking ticket I like better then you

You and that crack pipe gave me 'nough trouble—mor'n my share of pain
lickin' my ear—whisperin' your lies—pourin' my checkbook down your drain
I'm glad we spent time together—it always felt good between the sheets
but lovin' you's like payin' money to see a free dentist seven days a week

Hey, drag your laundry down Rose Avenue
then spend your time in your drugstore mind
it ain't what you think it's what you do
I had me a car wreck I like better n' you

Go ahead hock your stereo, sell your dog, there's always a new mooch you can find
maybe shack up with Al the bartender—he's got money—he ain't so picky —and god knows he's got the time
the good thing 'bout hurtin' this bad is knowin' some day it'll all be through
gettin' better might take some time but it's time I starter gettin' better over you

said gettin' better might take some time but it's time I started getting' better over you

SONG 2

Baby, when you need me and you're feeling low
and this fat old world is movin' too slow
ain't nothin' on TV and you got no place to go
why don't you pick up the phone and call me

And in your dark and your lonely room
where your loneliness is so thick you can eat it with a spoon
forgive me for what I done—let me come on home
Just pick up that phone and call me

When, at the age of forty-five
I started writing seriously
I'd been off booze for three years
and could finally sit in a room alone without attempting suicide

I gave myself a goal—one page a day
I would come home to my mom's house from the noon AA meeting
and write my one page

good bad or indifferent

that's how it started
one page a day
all I had to my name was my rage
and my father's temperamental old Smith-Corona portable

nothing else—nothing to lose
no apartment
no prospects for work
a piece-a-shit used car firing on seven cylinders
fifty bucks a week from Mom as a handout
and
my imagination
and
one desire—to be a good writer

now—eleven years later—no one can shut me up

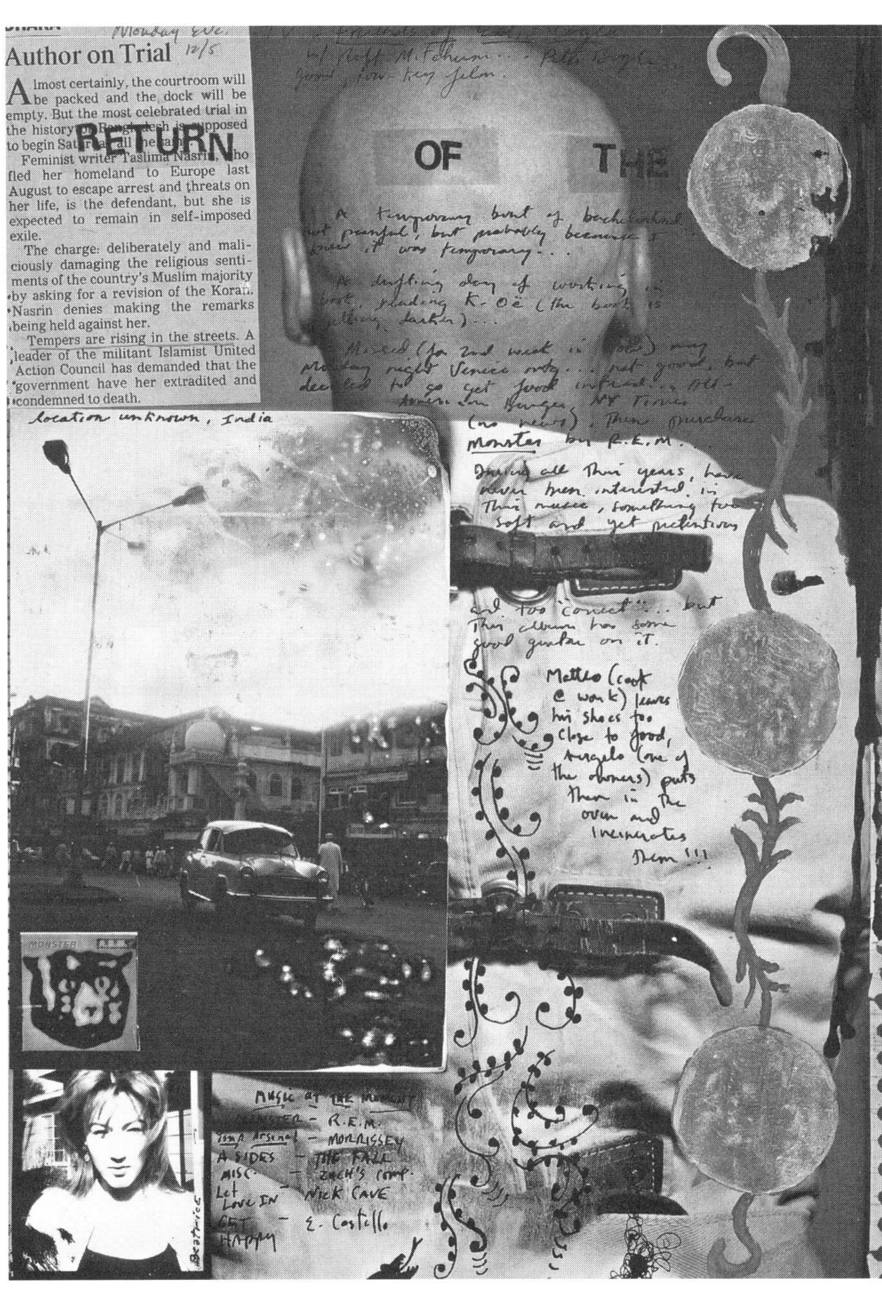

Monday Eve. 12/5

Author on Trial

Almost certainly, the courtroom will be packed and the dock will be empty. But the most celebrated trial in the history of Bangladesh is supposed to begin Saturday. [illegible]

Feminist writer Taslima Nasrin, who fled her homeland to Europe last August to escape arrest and threats on her life, is the defendant, but she is expected to remain in self-imposed exile.

The charge: deliberately and maliciously damaging the religious sentiments of the country's Muslim majority by asking for a revision of the Koran. Nasrin denies making the remarks being held against her.

Tempers are rising in the streets. A leader of the militant Islamist United Action Council has demanded that the government have her extradited and condemned to death.

My problem is
what I think

in my unmedicated mind

sometimes in bed in the morning even before my eyes open
they are there
the death squad
with
a
full hit list of my failures and my enemies and what I need to do to get
even
and who to call and what I'll say to the pricks to show them they can't fuck
with me

It just starts and proceeds—out of control—on automatic—by itself

Five minutes after I wake up—my life has spiraled permanently down the
shitter

And I am fed
whole and raw
to
the rancid wet crotch
of
another
day

BEVERLY HILLS

I found a teak-paneled bookstore
and under "F's"
I located *Collected Letters of John Fante*
(for some reason)
next to Bukowski

six crackling new copies

the cost of the book was over thirty bucks

"I guess you've arrived Pop" I heard myself say out loud
knowing
full well
the real price
for a true mad artist
is nowhere near
that cheap

6-11-93

L.A.

The long palms work their way
down Bundy Drive
swaying in the warm night wind
a chorus line of skinny hookers
nodding willfully
at the oncoming traffic
blowing kisses at Santa Monica Boulevard

Their cracked heels, unwashed arms,
and the heavy odor of the street
now hold no promises, no pleasures,
L.A.'s innocence is gone forever

I saw it once though
caught a glimpse
even said hi
waving out the back window of my parents' Plymouth
but it had already been bought and sold
and was much too much in a hurry
to stop
and say good-bye

6-18-93

A crazy Thursday night
driving the Malibu coastline for miles
heading north
a coffee mug between my legs
hugging the shore—sipping and smoking
escaping
wishing impossibly that I could somehow be a better writer
or less hopelessly bat-shit insane
choking to death on aloneness
on the thousands and thousands of words that have come from my
fingers onto the page—syllables with the smell of decomposing fish heads
and not
a-one worth saving

Stopping at dawn above the rocks
I got out of my old Pontiac
and watched the waxed waves come swarming in
unavoidable perfection reeking in
gushing in around me
drowning me

giving hope for everything—even a fuck like me

And—standing there—stupid
a fool with his dick in his hand
I knew once again
that all I had to do
was
shut up
and let it all happen

6-22-93

WE'RE REALLY WRACKED HERE

I tried affirmations
woke up early
hit my knees every day
willing to change, to do anything
begging to god or a chair or whatever else was out there
repeating over and over
words to shut up or shut out
the mad blackness eating away in my brain

It
didn't work
nothing stopped the bleeding

I did weekly drug treatment
and Rolfing, Rebirthing, Reichian Therapy
(that's just the R's)
overdosed
underdosed
and chanted until Yankee Doodle music came out my asshole

result: insanity 1, me zip

the last thing available
after more and more unendurable unending pain
at the last house on the last block
was
sur-fuckin'-render

that worked

7-1-93

For a long time I existed
in the darkness
preferring it

not needing to talk much or wanting friends
was easy

every sundown I'd come in and sign out, pick up my cab,
then follow the night
to get free
unplugged

year after year
rescued in a spacecraft drifting
through neighborhoods without faces and names

peace held me

so I could learn to feel myself separate from pain or need or judgment
and let the sweet wet streets lick my mind clean
like a lover

No great works were penned on those thousands of New York nights
no fortunes made, lost
but
best of all
alone
I got saved
rescued

from an endless night of pain

Saying I love you was not careless
for me
not frivolous
lots of gongs and horns have gone off before
and many wars . . . and years
have passed
where booze and blind need drove me
stalked me
then excused me
from sanity
and good judgment

here's the truth: most of the time it was my dick that was the problem

Now I don't care if I'm hot or cold
I expect nothing back
you can love me not love me
because—see
it's taken thirty years
but the voices—my madness—are gone
and
I've been given the gift
of
an inch
of
plain sight

JANUARY 8 SUNDAY 1995 8th day — 357 days follow

RAIN

Loungeing in early a.m. with Dipeaka... waking me up in the best way to meet the day that I've ever experienced...
Afterwards, some chai, lounging around waiting for a call from Swan re: mtg. for breakfast on this final day of her bros. visit (flight to U.K. @ 5:45 pm)... Penny calls... I'm not in the mood to either talk or listen, tell him I'll call him tomorrow a.m....
11:00 a.m. — Call to Swan, bros. are still packing and I work @ 1:00 pm., so the b-fast is out, agree to drop by on my way to work...

Swan's 12 noon

Bros are packing... maybe we just don't have that much to talk about, maybe they don't talk even with everyday friends... but, I have a hard time with the silence... I get antsy, morose, angry... "C'mon, let's at least pretend we care about what each other has done or that!"... This day seemed the... Swan but I didn't tell her I was tired...

...shower, dry off, then back in the car to get wet all over again. Sun roof leaks, driver-side window can't roll up... keeping in touch w/ nature is the way I like to think about it...

Eclipse of the ecstatic...

1 USSA
Serv... 3:49
2 BUDWE... 7.00
1 SMALL CE... SAL 4.50
2 RIGATONI ... 19.00
1 VEGETARIAN 9.25
2 SOFT DRINK 3.50
2 TIRAMISU 10.50
SUBTOTAL

Work drawing (Accidental "Kafka?)

Work

1:00 pm

— dead slow, but working w/ Ed, Scott, Amir kept me entertained... Break @ 4:00 pm. Pizza then a stroll up to Hennessy & Ingalls bookstore... Browse the illuminated manuscript section...
Back @ 5:00, still quiet, but biz. picks up, finally make a little money... off @ 10:00 pm... stop on the way home, call Dipeaka, go over for a visit... she's got those notorious shorts on that I gave her, and that fit her little butt so well that there's simply no resisting or controlling myself when she's got those on! But first, she gives me a present, a wooden printing block, used probably in decorating fabric or cloth, another tool for the drawings... Pretty soon, we're in her bedroom, back to where we began this morning... my god, intense, words fail me, besides, I can't go in to details, they're too delicious and nasty.

7-17-93

I discovered Van Gogh
about the time I gave up baseball
in Santa Monica
at a cheap picture-framing shop
with my old man
in back
flipping a stack of prints
while Pop argued over returning a chipped piece of glass

the pain in the paintings hit me like flames
jumped out
a mad man's hundred-year-old vivid fury
blasting me between the eyes
scalding my senses
and changing my life
like a first kiss

And today
driving
forty years later
I saw "Irises" again
in a window at a stop signal on Wilshire Boulevard

the light changed and behind me some dickhead began honking like a
fucking maniac
while I sat there wiping tears from my face
for the pure passion
in the vision of
Vincent's eyes

Today
my mind
that frenzied freeway nosepicker leering down a stalled 405
launching search and destroy
incursions
and
detonating hope at every off ramp

gave me something back

It was
an idea
and it came as softly as the lambskin seat covers
on the overheated Benz convertible blocking a center lane
paved by pain

My thoughts, it said
could
someday
—at all times—
be
my
friends

7-22-93

My old man's worst craziest most unreasoned passion
was for secondhand automobiles
he was known by every used car dealer on Santa Monica Boulevard as a grape
a mooch
and a sucker

for years half a dozen ill-gotten rusted junkers lingered abandoned behind his house
betraying him
banished from our family to the tall weeds
like so many derelict world War ll tanks poisoning the North African desert

Some of these preowned junk heaps would take no longer than a week or two to fail completely
ex-police cars, resprayed taxis
once he proudly pulled up our driveway with a coughing shitbox 20-year-old Ford then realized an hour later it didn't have windshield wipers or a radio

it was his curse
cars failed my father like faithless women

but he never gave up believing

and he always paid cash
and he always paid full price
for everything

[illegible]

[illegible] [illegible]

beautiful

ethical

a metaphor

Remember that Victorian Hotel
in Santa Barbara
the bedroom with the hundredyearold burl armoire
the overstuffed chair
and the sign that said "Beware of cat"

Having breakfast on the patio in the morning
guarded by too many sweating plants and trees
talking about our commitment to writing
art for work's sake
and you said, "Love wears well on you,"
and I said, "I'll lick you everywhere if you let me."

We paid up
and drove the slow way by the sea back toward L.A.

I still hated my poetry
but my tongue stayed coiled—patient and waiting
like a python
for the taste of you

8-21-93

I didn't study
(I was a backrow wise-ass Catholic school punk from jump street)
I hated all textbooks
with their tiny stupid words
packed together
pinching my eyes

Dirty little lower case b's and d's
and 6's and 9's and mn's and nm's and zy's izski's tortured me
driving me to failure

pages and pages of the fuckers

They dodged and squiggled and changed shapes
until I'd have to close one eye like a drunk
and trace line after line with my finger
letting globs of words ping ping ping away at my mind for paragraphs at a
time
until I realized
I had retained
exactly
zip

It's been 20 years since I've attempted reading any kind of
text book
or assembly instructions
or a warranty or a publishing contract

But
hey
when it comes to writing
the stuff where you say what's in your guts and in your heart
godamnit
I'll raise
my hand
every time

8-25-93

They know
the other 13 million grinding panicked type "A" L.A. minds
outside
in
the commuter freeway heat
with bumper to bumper needs needing fixing

RIGHT NOW

that life ain't fair

I mean who doesn't know that
a passing lane is always the answer
right?
finding that one single-minded goal that excludes all else
and provides the distinction between boredom
insanity
and
depreciation

first things first—I mean where's the fucking off ramp!!!

the confusion, of course, is in roadway selection

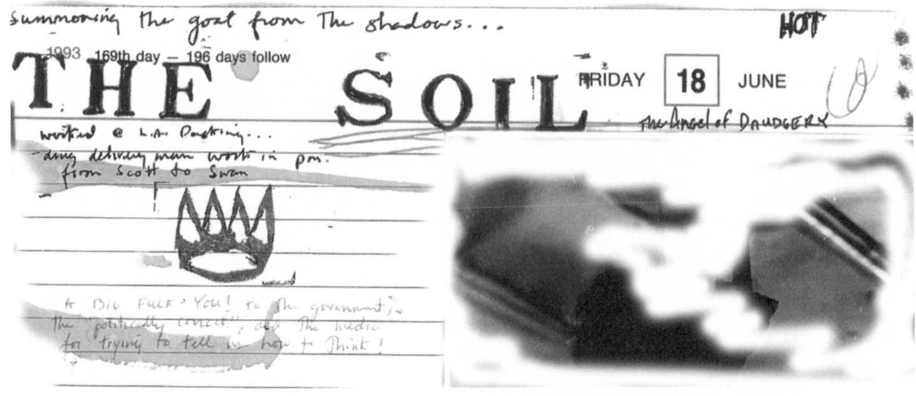

When I was done
screaming and snorting about who's in charge
and
about how being THE writer of THIS play gave ME a particularly singular insight and
that none of the emotionally-arrested ego-steeped actors in Act 2
could possibly fathom
in their teeny-tiny TV-commercial tits-and-ass audition-addled
childlike sunflower-seed-sized brains
the
extent of the emotions I had intended to be depicted
I
stabbed my finger in the air just to make sure that they knew
without question
that
I
have final say-so
anyway

(I mean you really gotta get this—they didn't understand!)

The leading lady put down her cigarette and her plastic coffee cup
looked at me sweetly with ageless bluer than blue
I'm the star of the show eyes
and
smiled

"There are 4.6 billion people on this planet"
she said
"and
at
any
given
moment
none of the motherfuckers is thinking
of
you"

Yeah—okay
so a kind of narcissistic madness is normal in Los Angeles
it is the way we think here
our
geographically skewed perception of ourselves
or
some-FUCKING-thing

You say "how are you" and my head says . . .WHAT DID HE MEAN BY THAT
or
. . . HOW DID HE KNOW THAT I'M FREAKING OUT INSIDE

see

I'm aware that the way my emotions work is not normal—I know
that's why I drank and in my own sweet time purchased 800,000 pounds of cocaine as an amusing distraction
and for years listened to this or that shrink tell me
where I'd overdone and overreacted
and isolated myself from sanity
I promise you I've discovered that all-important pivotal incident
(there were many)
in my childhood

so okay—
I understand

but still nothing changed

Let's be honest: every man has his own charter membership in the condition
the obsession of self-absorption
so it follows that sanity is separated only by
the thoughts
in
each
head

9-12-93

The hurricane was on the way they said—
hundred and five mile an hour winds
rain

wild shit—guaranteed

a great wet giant slogging across the Pacific to the tip of the
Sea of Cortez
about to spit cars and
uproot trees
and slap his red palms together
demanding attention like a bar bully pounding on the oak
demanding another drink
after last call

Everybody—
fishermen, tourists and residents
jammed the checkout lanes in the local market
like a casting call for frightened-looking customers

They boarded up our hotel while I sat at my typewriter sopping up instant coffee and watching the sea and wind do a twisted tango together

And I said to myself—I guess I'm ready for anything

except this

9-19-93

BASSIA

You're like a detached piece of me
reconnecting—
these days a voice on the phone
hoarse and crackling
after midnight and usually too much wine
out there
from some ancient location in tomorrow's time zone
Argentina or Spain or Egypt
Jesus, tonight it was a town
in Israel

remembering the magic we had once will never not
switch on the fire in my heart

I get swallowed
left drooling
with wondrous tales of this new place and that
the First Edition Knut Hamsun you found by accident
in that shitty bookstore in Edinburgh
or the business you'll start with so-and-so you met on the train from Berlin
or the saint you saw with hands bleeding
at Saint Damiano's in Assisi that changed your life forever—just last week

and too many cigarettes and not enough sleep
and missing your crazy daughter
and the poem I sent that you read just before you fell asleep on the plane
that time—and cried

A whole life—vivid as a technicolor kiss
reported back to me faithfully
each full atomic minute you've breathed in
picked clean
bursting and radiant

while I grope for a pencil—in my own bad light
—to write down the next
address
of the newest place that I will never visit
not even in my sweetest dreams

9-24-93

I watched with you
now fully domesticated
our bodies on the same clean sheets for hours . . . never touching
attention glued to the billion dots coagulating on the screen
celebrating the fluoride toothpaste genie, PMS, Ford trucks, anti-itch
cream, instant allergy relief, and fat Jenny Craig's mind-blowingly facile
recovery from Oreo cookies

—three pounds a week—guaranteed

and
I realized deeply—I truly mean this baby—I want you dead
I want to see you slashed open with a dull pocket knife
and watch a family of hyenas greedily gnawing out your colon
because see—thanks to you I'm now a fucking registered voter
my parking tickets are all paid
my drug dealers are all dead or in jail
and I've accepted the imperative of ending world hunger
and comprehensive health care

while I wait for the 11:00 o'clock news

344
If Griffith and De Mille believed in the power of spectacle, it took Welles to convince us that spectacle reveals its meaning, its full bloom, only at the moment when it rots and falls. That is why the figure of Falstaff swelled in his imagination,
Duttons Books
Browsing only... except I bought a book for Steve... is that thudding noise the sound of some one beating a dead horse?

After Arbus minus the infancy & drool....

10-3-93

John Fante visited me again this morning
made me feel his presence behind my writing chair
his warm breath

when I closed my eyes
I saw him
sitting at his writing table in Malibu
before his battered old typewriter
spitting out Tommy gun words and gulping coffee

and I smelled the sour stink of his Lucky Strikes
crushed out
and piled high on his ashtray stacked on two Knut Hamsun novels

and a new but ancient pain jumped out from inside me

Oh, Pop, (I even said out loud)
you ain't dead
I know it
just this second—in back of my eyes—
I saw you walking past me into the kitchen for another cup of coffee
or matches
and
I started to call out,
Hey Dad, didja hear, the Dodgers won today
or
I got an A on that history test

Oh Christ,
you're so here
right now
you can't have gone away

10-6-93

Across the street above the cliffs
I squeezed through the not-yet-electric-and-hooked-up
thick iron gates
to have a look

And there it was
in the cobblestoned courtyard driveway
still under construction
blocking even the moonlight
an immense three-layered marble fountain
still unoperational
twenty feet high with six (soon-to-be) water-gushing swans
looking inward
spewing rapture at a (taller than me) dickless gold fat-winged
baby cupid
balanced on one foot

Standing there looking up at him
in front of my mom's new neighbor's 5 million dollar
undecided
Renaissance Spanish Modern Italian outrage
overlooking Point Dume beach in Malibu

I thought
this is just what my old man moved from Hollywood forty years ago
to avoid

So I climbed up and pissed in the dry pond
and when I was done I tucked my dick away
zipped up my fly
and blew a kiss to cupid
and yelled out
for the benefit of John Fante's ghost:

Fuck you and all the Warner Brothers

10-8-93

You're not here
are you
baby
between you and me and your perfect naked nipples
are these needs of yours
that can't be put aside
and
when my tongue slips out from between your not-in-the-mood lips
I know
we won't be fucking again tonight
—you're too keyed up—
thinking about
this big deal or that
trying to reassure yourself
that you looked and acted right
at the meeting today to sign the contract that just may have insured your
district regional rep promotion

Look
I know you'll pick out the right dress to wear at the conference next
week
and make the payment for your red convertible on time
and send your niece her birthday card
but soon too
maybe tomorrow while you're on the phone
finalizing the details of some important contract
or charming the skivvies off a CEO
you'll find my note that says

so long Cynthia, I don't give a fuck anymore

Nonthinking things don't think
spiders and cats and a Portuguese chimp
they react
and life is decided
errorlessly
in the perfection of unknowing simplicity

not needing to figure shit out has envious symmetry
the instinctive awareness that the real music coming from the sound God makes
in empty hallways
barefoot
won't need explanation
or reassurance
or having to know where you can buy His latest CD
at a 20% discount

10-17-93

The goddamn rose bushes that came with the rented house
and the marriage
and the big back yard on Bundy Drive
that I told myself I was just testing out
now take up my free time most Sundays

Having been a bipolar pupil of bar stools and drunk tanks
and Reichian Therapy
these past years
unprepared me for the gardener's life

I was not always conscious of my crimes but sure of my guilt

Now I've discovered that a watering can makes a terrible tool for a suicide attempt

Fertilizer mixture and ample sun are my new concerns

I no longer need bail money
and I "act-as-if"
in old jeans and sweaty tee shirts
clipping this
transplanting that
and wondering how I got to be pruning flowers

unafraid and uncrazy most days

indifferent
as a geranium

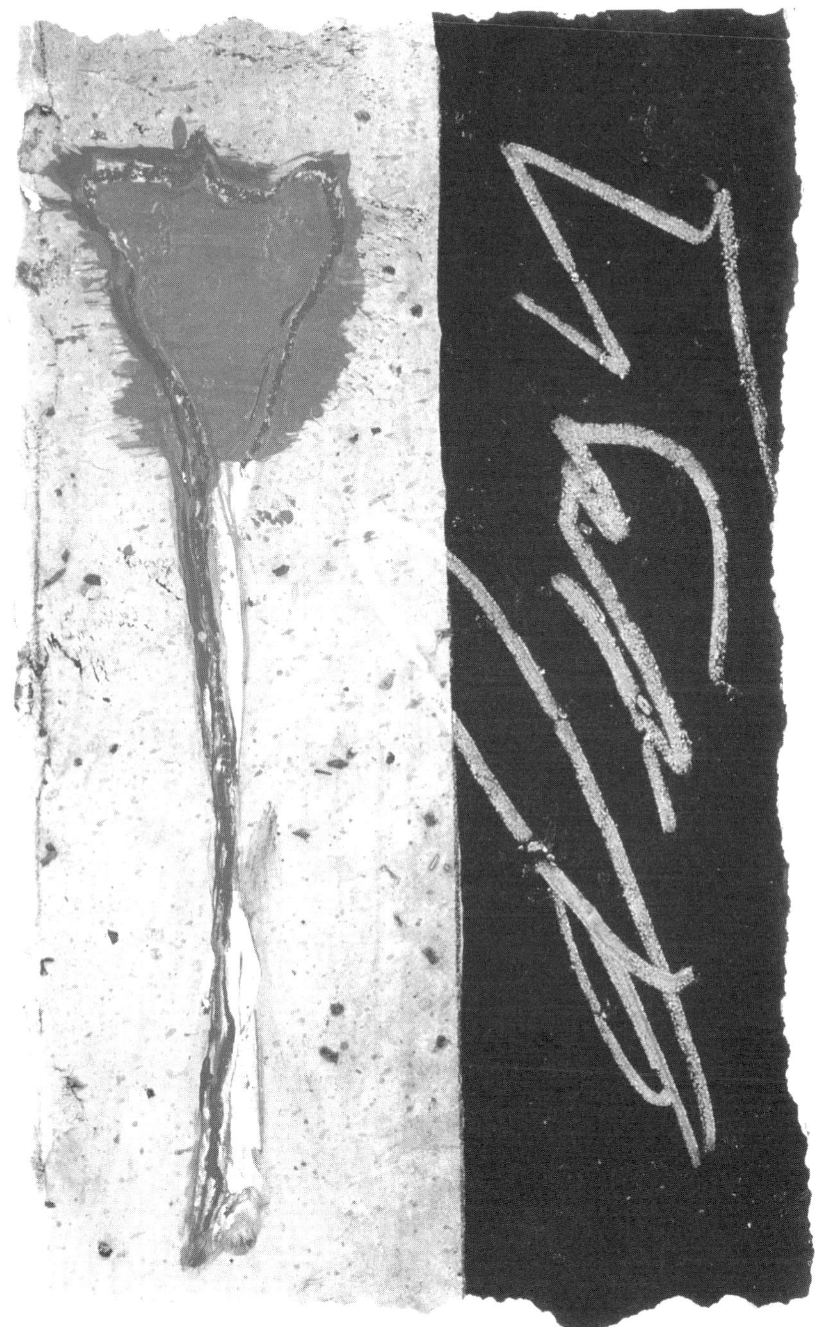

10-24-93

Maybe we'd just better kiss and let go
and you go your way
and me
mine

Maybe this deal has become too complicated
and the back-and-forth feelings too hard to heal

flipping lit stick matches at lakes of gasoline

I know I'm frequently wrong but never in doubt

We should just cash in
back off
be normal
and say good-bye

watching the *un*magnificence of one more explosion
is useless programming

the hell with this TV set

10-31-93

I bought a car today
my old one
the one that carried me through brokeness and depression
and attempted suicide
for years
complaining
but faithful as a wet stinking old dog
that would never give up or go home—
finally sprung a heavy oil leak
to go with the struts and the master cylinder and the radiator
that needed immediate attention
eighteen months ago

The smell of gasoline was making my passengers choke
at every stop light
and my new wife decreed that she would not ride in the beast ever again

So we stopped at a used car lot and I found a shining 3-year-old red one
(I always buy red whenever possible)
and said good-bye
and the salesman watched me as I put my hand on her trunk
and patted her
"Good-bye old car," I said. "You saved my ass over and over
and never quit on me"

Through the showroom window she was smiling
Approving
—a happy cosigner—

It was then that I grasped an immutable truth—
wives come and go
but a good used car
is a treasure

11-7-93

More often than not the barrel is dry
I sit there
a lunk—slurping coffee
correcting and recorrecting sentences
befuddled by my own odd childish syntax
missing the tone of the thing completely
discovering unhappily but honestly
that I was—no shit—better off driving a taxi

writing is pain for me—like rowing across mud
Phones ring
car alarms go off
dogs battle beneath my window
and after an hour's strain
pitiable
I sit and hold my head and have no notion why
day after day
I've committed my heart to such as this

Then
about one day in ten
gun loaded—100 Secanol and a water glass in front of me
the planets converge or some mishap occurs
and my stubby uncooperative fingers
for an instant—or half an hour
become mistakenly attached
to
the mind of whatever is eternal and magical
and
again
I feel the composition—the compulsion—of creation
and know
why
I keep on
with
this
madness

11-14-93

The most wondrous gift
I got
at ten
was Karen Birch leaning forward in the school bus
to pick up her books
her blouse flopped open
and ecstasy filled my eyes
like the tears Michelangelo had in his vision of the Virgin

I was immediately lost
mesmerized
carried to a place hidden in my head that has crippled and delighted me
these last forty years

I am dumbstruck by the miracle of women
again and again
rendered powerless
in the presence of a pair of perfect tits

7-29-94

I can clearly remember
all our issues
and arguments
like wet bread
on
a menu
that
turned out to be
layer upon layer of
so much
foul-tasting frosting

dontcha hate it baby when things go bad

after you'd worked
extra hard
meditating twenty minutes twice a day
overcoming incest
anorexia
and an inner child that lately
here
has grown fangs
and consumed what little love there was
left
over
after self-help

So okay
congratulations on your continued recovery

and I'll be sure to remember to sign the fucking divorce papers
next
Tuesday

An old yellow dog
lay by the back doorway of a restaurant
in the shade
on a mean August L.A. Monday

I watched him in the heat
from my writing window
as he baked motionless—stinging against the concrete

Joggers passed
coming down Bundy Drive
only two blocks—sports' fans—from where OJ sliced off Nicole's head and
let the blood drain giddily into her orphaned begonias

Sweating people got off and on busses at the corner of Wilshire Boulevard
a homeless couple—both men—overdressed drunk and dirty
(it took both of 'em to do it)
flipped over a massive green garbage can with a thud
searching for unwonderous buried treasure
while
airconditioningblasting
I dreamed of BEST SELLER blurbs
but stayed stuck
on a stupid rewriting of chapter 11 in my novel

Finally when the breathless sun reached his paws the dog did move
and I was sure by now my new soon-to-be ex-wife
had forgiven me last night's latest selfish infraction
and I made my latest vow to someday pay off the fucking IRS
and recommit to a new course of vigorous morning exercise

The yellow dog limped down the block and flopped safely in the shade
as a car honked at him and a dump truck shook past on Bundy Drive
and I sipped at the cold coffee
in my
half-empty glass

What happened
that I discovered symmetry
order
pure power
stars trusting their formation
and perfect terms of growth
balance
birth
and
death

Somehow I got located
picked out
and not randomly
had my trajectory tracked
to find me
fear filled
overpowered by need
flailing and screaming like a spoiled child
willing to trust instinct and fantasy
and even insanity
but never belief

So why now
this gift
after so much pain
this new life
this limitless smell of flowers
this bursting love
this sweetness that has overwhelmed my heart

Why me
special enough
to be
touched
by the hand of God

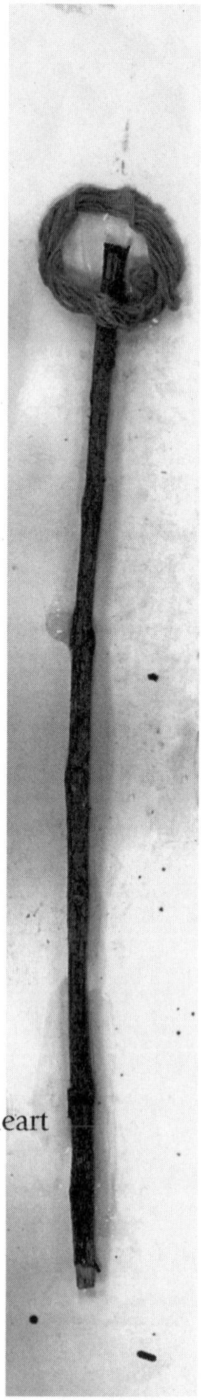

9-4-94

She taught aerobics Mondays Wednesdays and Fridays
I'd come by
and smoke
and watch her
and the others through the window
bouncing—dancing
firming up

my body was like Martha's
only without the elastic
and the sweat
and with thirty pounds more fat
but
we did hours in bed and I could never get enough
and she was a crazy mad bitch which is what heated my cock the most
always getting speeding tickets and lying about her checkbook balance
and owing everybody
and creating shit all the time and screaming at people in movies and
restaurants to be quiet then the next minute crying because the taste of
carrot cake was magic to her mouth

And I kept phone selling computer stuff to keep pace with her spending
diskettes and grosses and grosses of second-rate office supplies
and drinking like a slobbering dog all night
and
paying too much for this and that and going insane from the pressure
until
one monday
wild black-haired Martha was gone—packed up for good
her note said, "I'll call you, Danny-boy. I'm going to stay with my sister and
her kids in Bakersfield," which, of course, was just another lie
So that was that for the sexiest woman I ever knew
until
she came back
and
destroyed my life forever

9-4-94

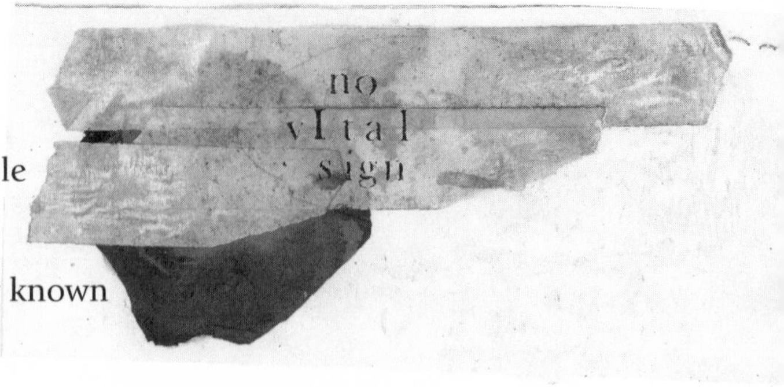

On my knees
I'm back
again
bleeding from every hole

I've forgotten
                    or never known
any peace anyway
and (truthfully)
out there
between me and the throbbing in my mind
there's just nowhere else to go

So turn on the TV
and call your fat-ass sister about that trip to Vegas
we talked about
and
change the sheets
and believe me when I tell you—no matter what—
no shit
no kidding
you're the honest-to-god
love of my life

At 6:00 a.m.
in sticky Milan
blurry-eyed
deeply jet lagged and
unable to sleep
about ready to read my stuff
and tip my hat
and—if possible
not pick my nose in public

all I really care about
on these trips
is not being exposed for the fraud that I am
preventing
at all costs
some half-drunk asshole guy in row three
from yelling up
hey moron, that's really awful—get off the stage

And me all the time
aware
of what he can't know
that the fear of being bad and being boring
in front of a lynch mob
is really what keeps any writer going
not the paychecks
or the reviews
simply just not looking dumb

Hell
all the rest of it is
luck
and smoke and mirrors

that's the real secret

They got Freetoz in the supermarkets in
Florence
and Dove soap
and electronic scanners
and checkers that grunt at you and don't give a shit
just like L.A.

And the guy standing on the corner
next to me waiting for the green
this morning on the Via San somethin'-or-other
was wearing a tee shirt that said NIKE
in big letters
and smoking a Marlboro filter

And I'm thinkin'
the enemy that I ran from
the one I flew six thousand miles
to escape
now resides
completely up my ass
and is located everywhere

I got so sickened by the thought
dehumanized
I had to stop
reach in my pocket—get my cell phone
and call my agent back on Melrose Avenue
to make him get the guy from Disney
on the horn while I hold
and tell him to go fuck himself
I won't take a dime less than seventy-five grand
for my screenplay

I mean
shit
we're talking art here
chrissake!

12-5-95

Fat saucer moon
be watchful
of those discount low-rent stars
like cheap electric
puppeteered
slippers
skipping across your sky
attempting
to entice
the untrained
eye

they're
jealous
thick moon
magnetized by something as beautiful as you

part of the chorus of vastness

substantiated evidence
that all perfection is a direction
that all we see and hear and touch and taste
and kiss
and resist

all

is part of
—not separate from—
the unblemished face
of
you

LA COSTELLA

Alone
halfway up the greenest green mountain in Italy
clicking photographs
and out of words
after rummaging through
a six hundred-year-old stone village
staggered by the uncomplicated power of what time has collected
here
shooing away angry chickens and generations of dust
but determined to wrap my American brain around
the experience of this place
what it means to be swallowed by my own history

I find myself
stumped
staring open-mouthed
like a child
in the presence of the these ancient damp rooms and rough hewn stones
they are like a tabloid headline from the renaissance
a lighted match
updating me to a revelation
the undeniable truth
that
I've caught
a glimpse
of God

ITALIAN LOVE

We met at the office
of my Italian publisher
Marco-the-Zap
me
back to Milano from a big reading in Sarzana driving all night
to avoid the summer heat

Stopped stone-cold by one smile

We are talking Italian pretty
here
with those amazing (look-out-baby-birth-and-death-is-on-the-way) eyes

Later, eating lunch in the restaurant with the rest of the office
the toothless old catso waiter humming a crazy version of—
of all things—"deep in the heart of texas"
I couldn't stop looking
and you couldn't stop smiling
and us both eating the same al pesto

Almost violently—right there in front of everybody
shocking myself— the bungi-jumping syllables wanting to leap out
(Jesus Mary mother of God
I have to kiss you and lick your tits
and get married tomorrow morning if you're not too busy)

But
instead
cleverly
saving the day
I asked
you
to pass the bread
instead

I always thought busy would stop it
or more exercise
or
costly blended whiskey
or a new red super-charged Chevy
or that falling down house I bought at the beach that time
or another marriage to a crazier bitch than the last one
or maybe a good review in *The Times*

but nothing stops it

nothing

stops
the
emptiness
of
being alone

The first time I heard
(Little) Richard Penniman
sing "Lucille"
wailing over the radio
I was a kid of 12 or 14

It was an amazing lightning rocket from Mars
a message as freeing and mystical
as
my first drink

I instantly felt
there was someone
a divine madman
willing to bet it all
to abandon himself
and fly out
as far as he could
to see the face of god

It changed my life in a wink

I met this American writer while in Milano
and we drank hi-test Italian coffee and ate dinner at an outside café
and discussed the wonderful vagaries of Italian women
in the summer night as they passed by
and he bought me a twelve thousand lira cuban cigar
to entertain me whilst we shot the shit
him talking and me catching

It came down to he was miserable
and pissing away his trust fund on his tall girlfriend
but convinced by his own brilliance
and education
letting me know that he spoke three languages
had a masters degree and had translated Dos-toy-fucking-evsky
but hadn't written a line on his five hundred page opus in two years

Halfway down my (free) cigar
and done with my third coffee
exhausted by this piffle
he wanted my advice
on how to make a commitment to his art

The only writers I know write
says I
carefully pushing my chair back to avoid any potential sucker punch
face the beast every day
and live and die giving birth to their stuff
but keep going anyway
until this thing they've borne and trapped and caged
has been fed all the raw meat it will eat and requests a toothpick

Writers who don't write, I said
are like hookers who don't suck dick
they should try new career choices
like flipping burgers
or the Italian post office

He didn't thank me or say good-bye
but
he did pay the check

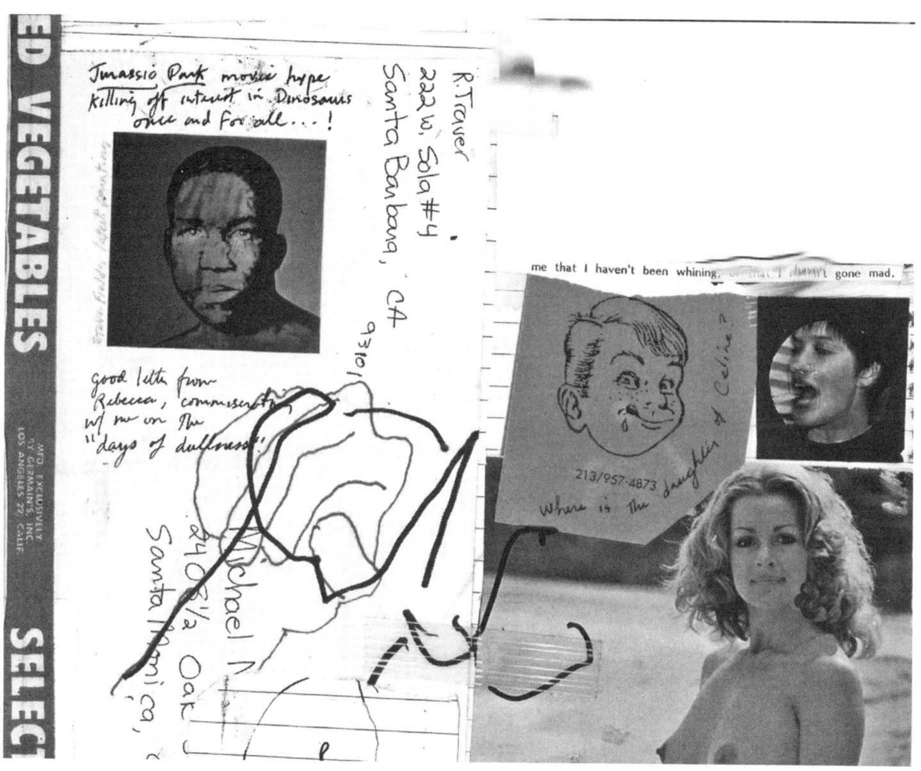

I don't talk about why I write
with people
because I'm still mostly unable
to do it
to really say
with humility
precision
and
intelligence
what really gets my dick hard about words

It always seems to come out egotistical or absurd or crazy sounding

So a while ago I gave up

But I'll do it now
here
alone in a room when no one can hear or see me
and I won't feel too much like a fool

My mission
why I write
is
to
change
the
world

Hey, don't laugh
I bet it's working

FOR LUCIA

After the heat
in the bookstore in Florence
where none of my books showed up for the reading
and
the craziest ride down from to the dripping hills
of Tuscany

In sudden seamless quiet
like spiders perched on the warmth of an ancient wall
we sat

Me
for once
out of words
childish and old against your beauty
smoking
allowing the measure of the night to perform
its music

Forgetting everything
except the syncopation
of silence
and the unexpected kindness
in
your
smile

For years
I poured bourbon on my brain
to kill the voices

but there came a time I had to quit booze completely
or check out

Some days it got so bad
I would have to pack up my shit in the middle of the morning
say I was sick
and leave my phone-sales job
very often
thirty seconds prior to a homicide

I'd stop off and buy two Big Macs and rent two porno movies
go home
pull the curtains
and pound the pumper into raw meat
hoping to shut the noise off

I needed hours of TV and 800 page novels and not answering the phone
for days
and not shaving or washing a dish
or changing my pants
just to stay even

Now
I've improved

and changed to Burger King

In the Pit, Dark Relics and Last Obstacles

JAN. 13 2002

Dream

There I was, super-urban, a man alone in the cold city moment, where I'm walking down the gritty big streets of what seemed like a combination of San Francisco and Manhattan (harkening back to my days living in the Mission District and North Beach... when I stop out of curiosity in a little market, inside an ancient jumble of the usual old market items (nylons, combs, old crackers) but over in the corner I spot and old revolving wire display rack with iron-on artwork patches, and they were the most beautiful abstract black passages, like a

Okay
so now *explaining*
is how you're going
to
change me

(pacing the bedroom within
your robe open and your glasses on your forehead
and your wonderful
center fold thighs
teardrop tits
and diet-pill stare)

Just now filled with some new pig-fat flash of mental espionage
some new truth
revealed
to you
this afternoon
by your knowitall two hundred-dollar-an-hour ditzed-out shrink
or Oprah
or a goddamn girlfriend at the gym

This need to make me really comprehend
for once and for all
in just six thousand short examples
what a selfish prick I am

And me
the dufus
laying here
in bed
a book on my lap
chanting for salvation
willing to pay any price
tell any lie
squinting at the shadows on your Sanskrit-motif-beige wall
hoping for you to

please shut up
so I can
just once more before I die or completely lose my sanity

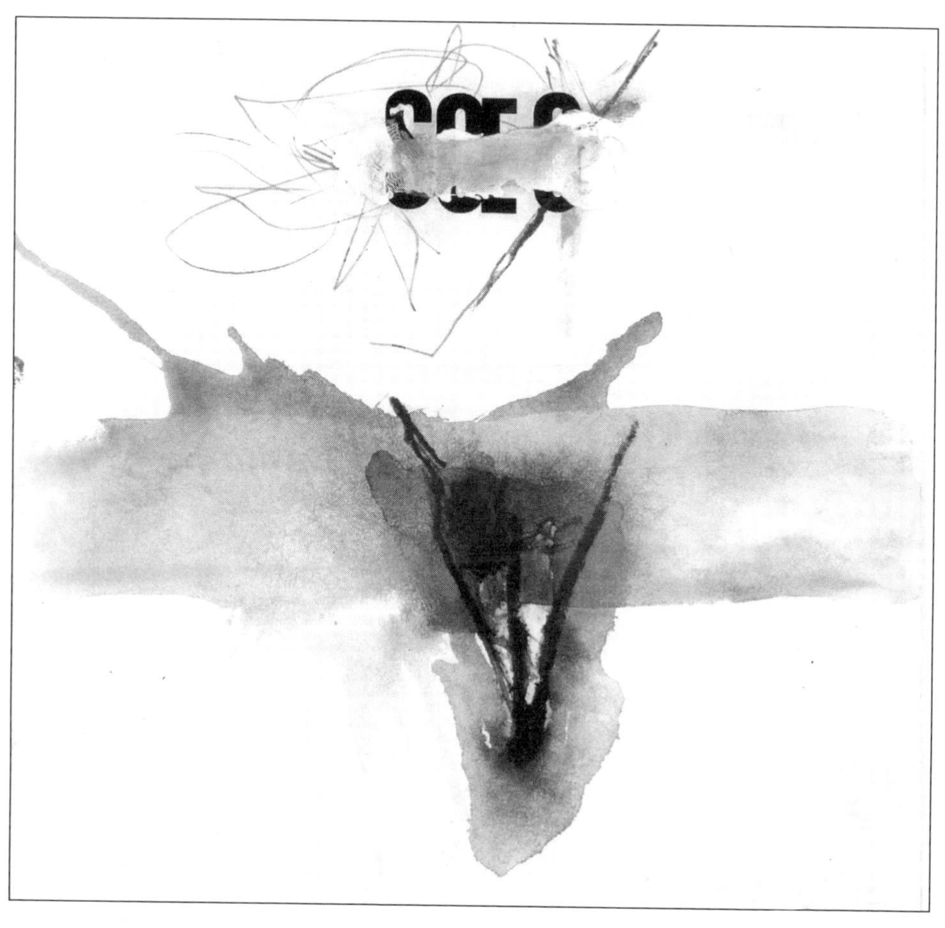

2

slam my dick inside the best
piece of ass I've ever had

I've fallen in love
regularly
twice a day
In Italy

I tell myself
Yo Pops
you're way too old
put your tongue
back in your face

And then
oops
there she is
buying cigarets
or
ordering coffee
some oozing black-eyed spectacle
in skintight pants

instant merciless come-fuck-me sex

I know there's incalculable history
here
I've touched it
my eyes and brain have absorbed
all there is
each molested molecule

But holy Jesus
help me
I'm drowning myself in these women

Everything in Italy
is a line

For trains
for first communion
for a newspaper
food
smokes
and busses

endless squishing and pushing

In Pompeii
I queued up for an hour on the cobblestones in the blazing summer heat
and listened nonstop to a babbling tour guide
just to step inside a suffocating stone room
for thirty seconds to see a 2000 year old fresco of a guy who
worshiped his cock

Now
days later
away from the frozen lava and the lines
safe at my keyboard
nothing blocking me but a blank page

come to think of it
why not—what else is new

he had the right idea

The kid upstairs
In apartment D
is crying
screaming unmeasurable survival syllables at the walls and out the
window
that
no one will ever decode but him

as I tap away
here
clicking out my words
flinging black dots at a screen
dots
dots
more dots

hoping to send some of this back to where we both came from

my own garbled transmission
this hieroglyph
to God

a thousand times less powerful than that kid's

but reminding me
that all I ever wanted
in my blackest nights
and most insane days

like him

was to fill the sky
with
my
voice

- make calls re: Chado next Sund

- call to Marvin
good chat, told me of Rebecca and him going to funeral mass yesterday for Anne Arone, the kids were there but her husband Joe is so far gone senility-wise that he doesn't even know of her death!!
Also, Marvin's going to look into co-signing a Visa/Mastercard for us for Phaedra.

"the first ready-made 1914, 'Egouttoir', galvanized rack for drying bottles"

... concerning the reconciliation of opposites...

3 SANTA MON... (310) 828
NTA MONICA
CAUTION: Federal law prohibits transfer of this drug to any person other than patient
R 427-734 R MONTEMARANO,
GISELLE NAPPER
TAKE 2 THE NIGHT BEFORE
APPOINTMENT AT BEDTIME THE
TAKE 2 TABLETS 1 HOUR BEFO...
APPOINTMENT
DIAZEPAM 5MG##
5 MG
R VALIUM 5MG
REFILLS

[ESK, qajaq]

...from the imperceptible writhing of a nerve-end, to the blinding white light of the cortex, where pain is no longer a bullying interloper in the body, but now is the body...

A walk down Montana Ave w/ Susan... no getting away from a Sunday... an acknowledgement of it is like staring into the sun; painful... a denial is like turning your back to it, a harsh sunburn on the back of the neck.

Waking up
back in L.A.
after a twelve city Italian reading tour
and twenty-two hours in planes and cars
my jaw aching
my cappuccino machine hissing and snorting
as I check three weeks worth of e-mail and phone messages
and shuffle through letters hoping for
any check
hearing my dentist's pissed-off receptionist
reminding me that I blew my root canal
appointment
again

Now
today
like the sweetness of a first kiss
after years of publishers telling me I'm unmarketable
and agents who've joyously refused my calls

I just realized

I'm making a buck
at the thing I love most in the world

I'm a real
no-shit
honest-to-Jesus
writer

My cappuccino maker went tits up on me
today
(the cheap Taiwan fucker)

It has saved my sanity these last eight months
but this a.m.
it crackled
and whirred and groaned
emitting the stench of electronic death
then quit completely

The guarantee stuffed in my drawer
says call the 800 number
so I did
staying on hold forty-five minutes
listening to light electronic subhuman snot

then
got
disconnected

Feeling all reason and sense oozing out my fingers
I watched my girlfriend move to the bedroom with a book
taking her fat kitty for protection
closing the door

Pants and shoes on
five blocks away
at Starbucks
waiting in line
for my fix
I coughed up the three bucks for a "tall"
then remembered
for a guy like me
a flat tire on the freeway
means
one of two calls at the emergency phone box

suicide prevention
or a tow truck

After my first novel
I took a break
and waited—drained
air and fire all ashes
after months and years of headfirst self-destruction
reenacted at a keyboard
by a ghoul alone in a room
painting his cadaver
applying powder and lipstick over the stab wounds
before viewing
the posthumous birth
of
a perfectly rounded turd

Every broken promise
the borrowed and unrepaid money
face after face dragged from the darkest rancid corner
of my gut

Open-heart surgery
for a writer

a kind of pre-death

requiring months of matinee movies
and TV
and books and weird sexual requests
just to recover
my chops

(AND THAT WAS TWO NOVELS AGO)

So
this week I get a fat envelope
from my publisher
with rave reviews
and high praise for my stuff from four countries

and a letter saying
stuff like
"we're on our way"

2

and
"from now on every book you write will ring the bell and reinforce
the excellence of your literary reputation"

As if what I have seething within me comes from a gleaming
oiled faucet
in the bathroom
of a hotel suite
overlooking
an impeccable Mediterranean June
and not from reliving twenty years of slow death

"Hey, thanks for your marketing insight"
my letter back said
"I'm done
I've decided to take up Chinese Checkers"

When I came back
the next morning
to our apartment
with the three-window view of Venice beach

shit was strewn everywhere

a hundred cigarette butts from upended ashtrays
broken dishes from our brawl
a cracked picture by the sink
her ruptured guitar face down against the linoleum

She wasn't there

but a guy was

sitting on the couch
a bottle of bourbon on the floor between his legs

"who're you," says eee
"Well—I live here," says me

Looking around
while he shook
trying to decide what I wanted
some keepsake trophy to commemorate six months of
SWAT Team mayhem
I saw Carver's short stories
laying on the nightstand next to the spermicide

Stuffing it in my pocket on my way to grabbing my razor
and toothbrush from the bathroom
I says at the door "okay, it's all yours"

"Any message for Randi"

"Yeah," I says
"tell her I'll miss the divine ocean air . . . and the teethmarks on my arm"

I sent a new play out today
stuffed the envelope
with a hundred clean and precisely typed pages
the way my old man taught me to do

spotless stuff
with a neat cover letter and return postage inside the envelope

and
as always
on my way home
the stinking black dog behind my eyes began sneering epithets

they'll never take it, asshole
it said
more time wasted and pissed-away postage
brainless inflated preposterous stupidity
you're a fraud—this time they'll see right through you for sure

Later
pouring coffee
looking out my kitchen window
on a wind-filled late-July afternoon

I remembered
that
years ago
sucking gin
living in that shithole in Venice
waiting
day after day
with the curtains drawn in darkness
and the TV with the sound off
owl eyes fixed on the line of light beneath my front door
how

my son-of-a-bitch brain was once armed and dangerous

I say
yes
to you too often
when what I mean
is
get away from me

My balls are eaten
like paté on Ritz Bitz
whole
in honor of my mock civility

duplicitous cowardice and falseness
is how I survive
relationships

Cast by the gods in the role of appearing interested
a simpering sound bite
when—all the time
in my
mind
I'm guzzling crank-case oil
and conjuring fantasies of twenty-year-old blow jobs

I'm your dishwasher (when you're working)
your dildo
your coconspirator
your gardener
a shit-house therapist
and a has-been author

a copayee in life's little stroll toward a dirt nap

whoopee

let's call
all
this stinking bilge

love

4-9-96

Three black guys in an open-bed truck
backed up on the lawn to get his stuff

the biggest of the three
the fat one
carried the thick old console TV single-handed
while the smaller guys pulled and dragged miscellaneous
boxes of shit
the dinette set
end tables—a bed—a bureau
pictures and a mattresses
away

It took over half-a-day—all told—this invasion
(me sitting at my keyboard—looking up from time to time)
and them
carting off the remains of the insensible old fool
delivering his life—a box at a time—to one of the dozens of used furniture
stores on Western Avenue

And I realized
when a man is really successful—when he's made his mark on the world
maybe they use
two
trucks

Publishers don't know what they're doing
not a one
and
trust me
literary agents know even less

I'm vexed by having these guys in my life
filling the earpiece of my phone
and e-mail screen
with
urgency
and diaphanous phrases
of tribute

truckloads
of sage pontifical market-driven
puke

When I hang up phone
or click off
I always know I've been sold a platinum toilet plunger
or fool's gold

white-knuckle applause

The only real peace there is for a writer is at the typewriter
facing it
as he must
headfirst
without artifice
waiting for the fingers to move
until
once more
with only the heart as a shield

he listens for the sound of the music

Snooping around
in the
poetry section
at Midnight Special Bookstore
I came on two thin
Ray Carvers

Flipped his pages
looking to find one
that exposed the poets heart
and passion
because with writers
feeling their feelings is what it's always all about

and Ray was good

What I got
after twenty trys
were polished stones
rather than
insights
and
the thought
that
Carver caught his last fish
set his final hook
at
not one second short
of
exactly the right time

Every writer should be that lucky

Part of writing
the kind of stuff I write
is
gaining a reputation as a disgusting deviant diabolical dope fiend
and alcoholic madman

Well, there are no points for style

Having stuck my dick
in all manner of moist
breathing and nonbreathing orifices
merrily coupling with man and beast alike
and been diagnosed addicted, insane, schizoid, antisocial
with a dash of clinically depressed
and
having ravaged my friends and enemies and their wives
and
stolen
lied
cheated
and misappropriated whatever suited my fancy

Then having been confined kicking and screaming in jails
from Texas to the Tombs in New York
and attempting to off myself countless times
in blackouts
or wide awake with a gun or a razor blade in my hand

I'm here to tell you
it was all me

a slice of life done with bells clanging and whistles tooting
my own personal little journey to find God

So guess what
here's the kicker

it was all worth it

×7
The Self
God

I'm moving to Tibet
I'm disgusted
tired of the drunks screwing with me on the
Venice streets
of going into a 7-11 and discovering that
I'm the only one who speaks
the mother tongue
and traffic

And overextended plastic
and multiplying IRS debt
for my years of thoughtless deadly omissions

This day-by-day survival in extraordinary
American madness
where my vote don't mean nothin'
and the candidates
are morphed by greed
and the only choice is more and more
TV mentality

Dots pile up on my pages like
sans-serif DOSS boat people
praying for a pay check

I don't care
none of it matters
I'm off to Tibet
or Pluto
or Bakersfield
to locate God

up my asshole

FOR NICK

Mom dressed me
in new blue jeans and a clean shirt
and combed my wild hair down
and made me wait on the road
next to you

I was sure my chest would explode

Everything that ever broke in my life
seemed to be broken that day
each memory of stupidity and confusion
my lies and crushed toys
the time I poisoned the cat
or crapped in my pants and couldn't tell anyone
or smashed Dad's electric razor
into a zillion tiny plastic bits

It was all there
the day I started school
pure panic rendering me speechless
sitting next to you on that bus

My big brother
holding my hand

not caring you looked like a goof

telling me not to cry
it would all be okay

Well, it never was
Nick
I never fit in
and hated every minute of the next 14 years in school
and would have preferred a spear through the neck
but thanks anyway
for trying

A pretty girl I met in
Milan
who'd read my books and has seen me do my writer act
and drank coffee with me
and shot the shit
sent me a surprising e-mail today

It seems we are metaphysically connected
soul mates and
the air she breathes is filled with gusts of my words
and the smell of my sweat
and pain
and
according to her
our spirits travel as one through some star-stormed galaxy of love

She informed her boyfriend
about our love
blurted out the truth in tears
after a good roar in the rack
and
naturally
it's all okay with him
he understands our *connection*

After I clicked off
I treated myself to a fresh blast of espresso
and a shave
squinting at the old dog in the mirror
who'd been waiting
minimum
10 years for a note like this

Art has it rewards
thought I
not the least of which
is
a woman's small kindness
and the best coffee
a buck can buy

Today
my niece
called
and arrived
in L.A.
breathless
ten days short of her eighteenth birthday

Her pops, my brother Nick
now three years in the ground feeding worms
after a lifelong betrothal to his Beefeater bottle

The kid wants to see Venice Beach
and test her hormones on local dance floors
visit tattoo parlors
and watch tanned bellybuttons being pierced
while she flaunts her long red hair on the endless California beaches

ah, to be eighteen
in the blue sky of July

As far as I'm concerned
I'd rather
stick a straw in a quart bottle of
antifreeze
& then reunite
with
her dad
in the big 4-point restraint whack-ward in the sky
than
B
that young
again

I want to be dust
when
I'm done
pulverized and exhausted by my own sweet madness
I want laughing and telling stories at my wake
and Groucho Marx glasses on my white corpse
and
I want someone saying
with a grin
"this guy's flame was totally used up"

I want a fistfight
and two crazy drunken bitches
arguing
and to hear Little Richard
screaming "Lucille"
while they roll my coffin toward the fire

I want it known that through chaos
I found my voice
And in pain I found a fresh birth

I want to hear dogs barking
and tires squealing
I want life to go on and on and on without me

I want dripping cotton candy
and the smell of my woman's dirty underpants
and
I want it known
that the smiling overpaid old devil
in his lined satin box

had the most swell fucking day

need
is
a frantic mad scream

produced

from
no place
near
God

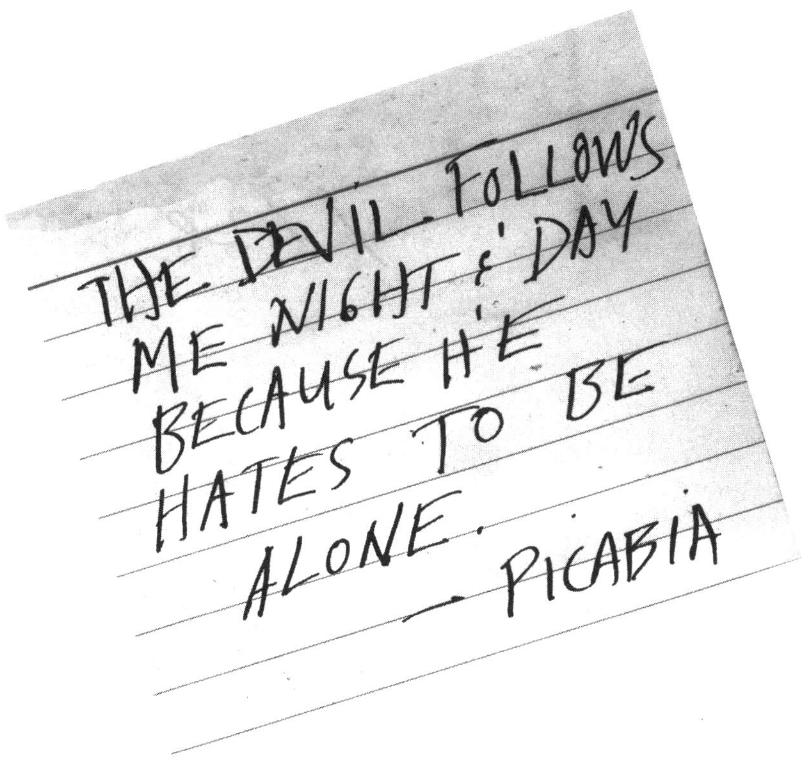

White crisp sheets
float me
and
the sweetness of you
is there
enduring
half an hour after you've gone
towing your glow down the Coast Highway
in
your yellow bug and fitted teacher's suit
protecting
the slut hidden within your bikini panties

All red hair and green eyes
and perfect teeth
teaching kids to love words

leaving me

hugging the sanity of Hemingway
with orange juice in bed at 7 a.m.

I didn't get here on a winning streak
and I'll never know how I earned the tribute of a duplicate house key
with my moods and rages and mechanical insensitivity

What I really deserve
I never got
a team of guys in white jackets toting garbage bags
picking up chunks of me
from a smoking crater half a mile wide

I guess I'll have to settle for this
and
quit my bitching

It was ripped
from me
unknowingly
by my own hand
and
I bled salvationless oily useless tears
trying to get it back
but nothing and no one can replace what has been lost

only the self survives

Innocence has to be unlearned by pain
then
experienced again
like a fresh piece of ass

I will fall one day
and a dump truck with two guys
wearing ragged overalls
will stop and scoop me up

They'll carry me off to cold storage
painting my face
making my teeth look straight and white
before
they ignite my useless bones

My ashes will be thrown in a park somewhere
under a tree
and little girls wearing oxford shoes
playing jump rope
will bounce up and down on wisps of me
until they begin to dream of boys
and discover bras and thonged pink panties
and the secret pleasures to be found when no one is watching

All this will delight me no end
and somewhere
in eternity
jerking off
I will experience unremitting contentment

MAY 2 8

?

DESTROY ALL SLACKERS

lom
ad
becca
ndra (52 pick-up)
nt Ruby
e: Flossie
e Ortiz
ny: Richard
is Toledo
gy (braces)
y Sample
Brazil
Ann
ia Eddington
yn Miranda
Hasty
Senner
chleys
lemons

hen
Smith
Impastato
y Hartford
Miss Maramoto
Steve Weiss
Steve McKay
Steve Behrens
Kyle Loestner
ile
shing
ld
d
ylists..
seem
e days,
hing
ions
oned
lorishes,
awhile,
hen

Bill Musick
Steve Musick
Mike Tapia
Steve Tapia
Ed "Big Daddy" Roth
Father Adam
Father Louie
Suzy & Tessie
Gypsy
Cheryl Tengan
Debbie Buford
Heidi Fallon
Jo Ann (friend of Heidi's)

Neil Young
Felix Pappalardi
Ian Anderson
The Kingsmen
Lou Reed
David Bowie
T.Rex
Iggy Pop
Ray Charles
James Brown
Wolfman Jack
Roy Belosic
Diana Ross
Martha & The Vandellas
W.C. Fields
Marx Bros.
The Untouchables
Naked City
hnny C.

Chris Walle
Forest McFarland
Johnny Fram

Andy Warhol
Tom Sullivan
Bianca Jagger
The Stones
Victor Hugo
Chanel
Sander
Jos. Beuys
Morris Louis
Paul Klee
Claes Oldenburg
Alan Kaprow
Jim Dine
Rebecca
Penny Travers
Bill Mast
Ray McClean
Ray Kennedy
Dennis Kennedy
Paris Vaughan
Tom Huston
Serena
Loni Sanders
Dominique Simon
Ava Jacks
Leslie Forester
Herman Hesse
E. Hemingway
Faulkner
Paul West
J.K. Huysman
Knut Hamsun
Gunther Grass
Heinrich Boll
Rachel Amodo
Debra
Vera Ingrassia
The Fall
New Order

Jobs and fortunes
are won and lost
and so it goes

kids grow up
copying the mistakes they've been shown
and so it goes

Fools run nations
campaign again and get revoted in
and so it goes

Stupidity is recycled
like homogenized snake venom
and so it goes

The greatest fortunes
are won and quickly pissed away
and so it goes

History repeating itself
coming first as tragedy then as farce
and so it goes

Until some fool has horse sense enough to step out of the fucking line

That soft
place
the gentle inside of your thigh
like the cheek of a flower
and
then the tangy-stinging-taste of you
opening on my tongue

that flawless first time

like the sweetness in waking and sleeping all at once
or
when I was five—knowing and feeling the amazing magic of the calliope
on the carousel at Santa Monica Pier
safe in my dad's thick arms going around and around forever

nothing
except you
and that feeling
has ever been more perfect

3-31-2000

I saw a guy check out
just before lunch—today

Waiting for the crossing light on the corner of Wilshire Boulevard
a bad paperback and my newspaper under my arm

I'd smoked my cigar and sipped my snazzy Starbuck's coffee
and exchanged chitchat with Ann the counter girl
with the "D" cup—about the odds of her leaving her old man and running off to Mexico
with a swashbuckler like me—and
made a fresh resolve to start another novel
then knew immediately it would go the same way as the rest of my tedious, worthless shit
these days
and

ultimately

change nothing

Then
hearing this hellish noise
I look up
to see metal flash and spinning red
and another car hit that car and that car crash into a concrete pole
and the body of this business guy—headfirst—his paisley tie and 3-piece suit still correct and in place—
explode through the front windshield
of his SUV on a nonstop trajectory for an 11:07 a.m. face-to-face appointment with Jesus

And half an hour later—at the secondhand bookstore on Santa Monica Boulevard—it came to me—maybe stupidly
that this guy won't be going for a run after work today
or returning the urgent phone call from his broker
or kissing his kids good night
or doing whatever it is people do
before they die abruptly beneath a flawless April sky

4-16-00

Opening the *L.A. Times Sunday Book Review*
today
I saw it
three
full pages
about John Fante
my
old pop

consensus wisdom has now pronounced absolute praise for a new
national treasure
a biography is out about a passionate, crazy, drunken, angry
L.A. writer
a volcano of a man

and
instead of being happy for my dad
I sat furious—the words tore at my heart
and
I yelled something shitty at my girlfriend down the hall in the bathroom
about her cold coffee
and I thought fuck the fucking *L.A.Times*—they're fifty years too late
it can't help him now
he lost and gave up
blind and in a stinking hospital ward where the night maintenance guys
kept stealing his radio
and the Dodgers had their worst season in years
and I remember
sitting with him and holding his hand to my cheek and thinking to myself
what a lousy way to die
for a man who once had such power
whose words held so much beauty
that the sky itself
was increased by a billion stars

2002

Now that I've written
ten years worth of books and plays
and given up booze
and cigarettes and filthy glorious pornography
and my clothes don't stink from sleeping in my old Pontiac all night
and my hair is thinner and I'm twenty pounds too fat
and deep in my fifties with return calls to make and responsibilities
and the arguments I have with cops are no longer about bail and unpaid
warrants or where I hid my gun
I
now feel qualified to testify that time has changed nothing
this thing that all my life within me has ticked and squirmed
—this unfilled hole
—this need to yell out and to change things and never be satisfied—
this voice that has survived shrinks and jails and 3 divorces and suicide
and bankruptcy and dozens of self-improvement weekends
this rage
still guides my vision
and demands that I go headfirst against my life
like a fool
in search of
a
pure
white
flame

To Mark

Walk with only words
and books
as your friend
dream the dreams of deviant dead writer saints
who
coming before you
drowned the pain of their purest heart
in vats of gin
like a flailing
unloved cat

Embrace selfishness
and joblessness
smoke millions of unfiltered cigarets
and glue your ass hopelessly
to the evilest drunken crack whore
who'd trade your balls in a New York instant
for the guy at the end of the bar
with the pitted face
and
a fifty dollar bill

Do not be courageous
remember that all men are fools
and liars
soulless captives of their own bloodstained necessity

and forgive nothing

Then maybe one day
like me
your feet aching and your skull still raw from last night's festivity
you'll kick over a box
or turn a page
and find yourself face to face
with
the blurry eyes of God

Books by DAN FANTE

Les anges n'ont rien dans les poches (1996)
Chump Change (1998)
en crachant du haut des buildings (1999)
Angeli a pezzi (1999)
Mooch (2000)
la tête hors de leau (2001)
Spitting off tall buildings (2002)
A-gin-pissing-raw-meat-dual-carburetor-V8-son-of-a-bitch from Los Angeles (2002)

Books by SUN DOG PRESS

Steve Richmond, *Santa Monica Poems*
Steve Richmond, *Hitler Painted Roses*
(Foreword by Charles Bukowski and afterword by Mike Daily)
Steve Richmond, *Spinning Off Bukowski*
Neeli Cherkovski, *Elegy for Bob Kaufman*
Randall Garrison, *Lust in America*
Billy Childish, *Notebooks of a Naked Youth*
Dan Fante, *Chump Change*
Robert Steven Rhine, *My Brain Escapes Me*
Fernanda Pivano, *Charles Bukowski: Laughing With the Gods*
Jean-François Duval, *Bukowski and the Beats*

This first edition is published in 1,000 hardcover copies, with 226 numbered and lettered copies signed by the author.

Thanks!!

#36